C000212870

Relativity

PATTI HARDESTY

AuthorHouse™
1663 Liberty Drive
Bloomington, IN 47403
www.authorhouse.com
Phone: 1 (800) 839-8640

© 2019 Patti Hardesty. All rights reserved.

No part of this book may be reproduced, stored in a retrieval system, or transmitted by any means without the written permission of the author.

Published by AuthorHouse 03/14/2019

ISBN: 978-1-7283-0414-4 (sc)
ISBN: 978-1-7283-0415-1 (hc)
ISBN: 978-1-7283-0413-7 (e)

Library of Congress Control Number: 2019903002

Print information available on the last page.

Any people depicted in stock imagery provided by Getty Images are models,
and such images are being used for illustrative purposes only.
Certain stock imagery © Getty Images.

This book is printed on acid-free paper.

Because of the dynamic nature of the Internet, any web addresses or links contained in this book may have changed since publication and may no longer be valid. The views expressed in this work are solely those of the author and do not necessarily reflect the views of the publisher, and the publisher hereby disclaims any responsibility for them.

authorHOUSE®

Dedication

This book is dedicated to my son, Matthew. He is the joy of my life.

Acknowledgments

Many thanks to Matthew Hardesty, my son, who gave great attention to photographing my art work for this book. Also, my everlasting gratitude for his constant support and encouragement throughout this process and always.

Contents

Mother, You Are Like a Willow

Mother, you are like a willow

Whose forlorn beauty haunts my soul.

Tendrils tangling in angry tempests,

Then gaily dancing on a breeze.

Drooping limply in the doldrums,

But offering a shady rest,

Shelter from life's elements.

Appearing deceptively weak and fragile,

But strongly rooted in the good earth.

Bending,

Never breaking.

Aspens

Rehab Romance

Against the odds,

Against advice,

Against the rules-

It wasn't wise.

They took a chance.

They went all in.

They had romance-

They HAD to win!

They were in love,

But still committed

To staying straight-

They weren't dim-witted!

Somehow they both jumped the track.

Now, they won't be coming back.

Both are worse off, but never mind.

Love is deaf and dumb and blind!

Cock of the Rock

Letting Go

It's very difficult, you know,

To learn the skill of letting go.

The lost cause, the hopeless dream,

The endless battles may all seem

Easy things to lose hold of.

But losing you,

Losing your love

Is harder than I ever

Imagined.

What I've Found

What I've found

In your smile

In your eyes

In your voice

In your touch

In your arms

In your mind

In your heart

Is every thing

I could want.

Dreamboat

Dream Sweet

Now I lay you down to sleep,

I pray the Lord your soul to keep.

I kiss your face, your hands, your feet.

My precious baby,

Dream sweet.

While the world is spinning round,

The house is dark, there is no sound

Where love and joy and contentment meet

In my little angel-

Dream sweet!

Flying Solo

I went into your room last night and called your name.

Could you hear me?

I smelled your pillow for your familiar scent,

But it has faded.

I touched your favorite books and mementos,

Keeping them exactly as you had left them.

This empty nest is so quiet

Without you,

But I know you have to try your wings,

And fly solo.

Why Worry?

I worry because

you need me.

You need me because

I love you.

I need you because

you love me.

You love me because

I worry.

I love you because

you love me.

You love me because

I love you.

Why worry?

We just need to love each other.

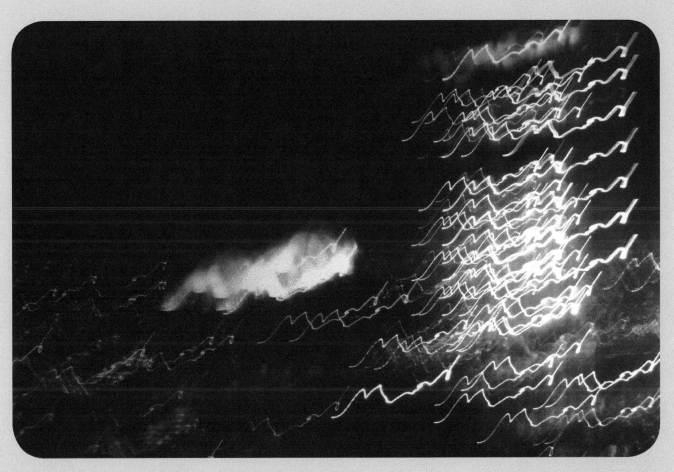

Ghost of New York City

Brilliant

Brilliant you are-
A flash of light,
Focused energy
Shining bright you are-
Smart,
Edges sharp.
Sparkling you are-
A star,
A gem
So priceless you are-
Of inestimable value
To so many.
A treasure you are-
Enduringly,
Amazingly,
Brilliant.

Duty

I know about duty-

I do what I must

Til ashes are ashes

And dust is dust.

I believe in commitment,

In standing by

The promise we make

Until we should die.

To not run

When it's no fun,

In health and sickness,

Through thin and thickness.

When age is gaining

And passions are waning,

It's how it should be-

Just you and me.

Blue Lady

Sometimes I Cry

When I'm all alone
And nobody's home-
Nobody comes.
When I'm sad inside
Going out with the tide-
Nobody comes.
Sometimes I cry.

I have friends, but where are they now?
There's no one here for me anyhow.
Nobody comes.
Sometimes I cry.
Sometimes I cry.

I can't get off the merry-go-round.
I have to go on riding around.
Nobody comes.
Sometimes I cry.
Sometimes I cry!
Sometimes I cry...

Too Sad to Think

It is too sad to think
That I will never see you again,
So I pretend that I will.

It is too hard to believe
That anything really matters,
So I pretend that it doesn't.

It is too risky to feel
Love once more,
So I pretend that I don't need it.

But I won't,
And it does,
And I do.

Pumpkinshell

This Old House

This old house has a heart and soul.

It held my family when it was whole.

My son has grown and moved away,

My husband died on Labor Day.

Now I rattle around in a too big shell.

I want to stay, but I need to sell.

This house needs a family and fun,

Kids in the pool, and teens on the run!

A dog in the yard, and a cat on the chair,

Great food cooking- good smells in the air!

It should ring with laughter and beat with love,

Keep being blessed by God above.

So, I guess I'm ready to say farewell

To this old house I've loved so well.

Absinthe

Old Friend

Hello, friend from long ago!

I had not forgotten, though

We have not spoken in many a year.

I am still yours.

I am still here.

Much has been lost along the way,

But we are still in the fray.

We speak of friends and days gone by,

Those no longer living-wondering why

We have survived.

I think I know.

We snuck out the window and traveled far,

Took trips without leaving my room- no car.

Sticky Fingers and Aqualung (our friends were shady).

We knew very well the Green Eyed Lady.

Our carefree days of youth soon became

Births, marriages, deaths,

Secrets, lies, and blame.

We grew up too fast-

But that's what we wanted!

We were young.

We were strong.

We survived-

Because that is what God wanted!

Mosaic Bowl

Fusion

I dream of Dichroic hues-

Vibrant colors,

Rich and deep

Infuse my sleep.

Iridescent remembrances that change,

Even as you gaze

Simply amaze

My friend and I-

Designing adornments.

Summoning spirits for inspirations

For our creations.

Nippers taking bites of glass,

Cutters scratching lines that break

Perfectly when pressed with precision.

Each act an important decision.

Arranging organic shapes just so,

Applying intense heat

To meld and transform

A unique piece is born.

This is Fusion.

Eye of God

A Modern Psalm

You are the solid ground my foot finds

When waters are rising all around me.

You are light in the darkness-

There is no need to fear the shadows.

You are peace in the midst of turmoil,

Reason in the face of anger.

You are my joy.

You take away my sorrow.

You are hope of a better tomorrow-

Forgiveness for all of my yesterdays.

I am done with pleasing others, even myself.

I only need to please you.

You are all I need.

All I need is you.

The beauty you create is beyond human imagination.

Your power is limitless.

Your love is unfathomable.

Help me to do your will, Lord.

I am your servant.

Amen

Rooted

Autumn

I am in the Autumn of my life-
My favorite season.
I love the crisp, cool days,
The achingly beautiful blue skies.

Autumn always makes me nostalgic,
Recalling Autumns of the past.
I find myself taking stock,
Remembering times both good and bad.

Life is achingly beautiful now in many ways- Not perfect,
But I appreciate things more now.
I am savoring this season before Winter comes,
Trying to prepare for the colder times ahead
By working on ways to keep warm (in my heart).

Love Comes to Stay

Love can find you when you least expect it,

When you're tired of trying and feel rejected.

Love can catch you when you're running blind,

When you've given up and you're out of your mind.

It happens right before your eyes,

A new light dawns and you realize

That love has come to heal your heart.

Love has come to stay-

And may it never part.

Here's to Love

Here's to life-

Fill your cup!

Here's to love-

Drink it up!

God is good-

All the time!

I am yours-

You are mine!

Here's to life-

Fill your cup!

Here's to love-

Drink it up!

Relativity

Relativity

If I died today, I would want to be remembered as follows:

I hope my son would say that I was a loving mother.

I hope my mother would say that I was a caring daughter.

I hope my husband would say that I was a faithful wife.

I hope my brothers would say that I was a supportive sister.

I hope my friends would say that I was a loyal friend.

I hope my patients would say that I was a compassionate nurse.

I hope my students would say that I was an inspirational teacher.

I hope all the people I care about would say that

I let them know that I loved them,

And how much they meant to me.

This is a life well lived.

It is not about accomplishments.

It is about relationships.

Most of all,

I hope my God and Creator will welcome me home with open arms.

CPSIA information can be obtained
at www.ICGtesting.com
Printed in the USA
BVHW021041210319
543335BV00014B/157/P

9 781728 304151